Georgina Phillips studied design before deciding that being a writer would be easier and more fun. She worked as an in-house copywriter before going solo in 2000 and now writes for museums and galleries on topics as diverse as war, outer space and food. She has one daughter and lives in North London. She hasn't endured anything very tough at all in her life but is full of admiration for anyone who does. This is her first book.

WOW!

Alan Rowe was told by one of his teachers at school, when caught drawing silly pictures in his maths exercise book, that he'd never earn a living drawing silly pictures. Since completing a degree in silly drawings, at Kingston in 1985, he has been doing just that.

weird!

He has a silly partner, who also draws silly pictures, three very silly children, two silly cats and lives in a silly place in Surrey . . . seriously.

Also published by Macmillan

THE ULTIMATE SURVIVAL GUIDE FOR BOYS
by Mike Flynn

YOUR PLANET NEEDS YOU!
A Kids' Guide to Going Green
by Dave Reay

SPYMAKER SPYING CODEBOOK
by Sandy Ransford

SPYMAKER SPYING HANDBOOK
by Sandy Ransford

the science of...

ouch!

eXtReMe
feats of human endurance

GEORGINA PHILLIPS

Illustrated by ALAN ROWE

MACMILLAN CHILDREN'S BOOKS

First published 2008 by Macmillan Children's Books
a division of Macmillan Publishers Limited
20 New Wharf Road, London N1 9RR
Basingstoke and Oxford
www.panmacmillan.com

Associated companies throughout the world

ISBN 978-0-330-45405-6

1 3 5 7 9 8 6 4 2

A CIP catalogue record for this book is available from
the British Library.

Typeset by Nigel Hazle
Printed and bound in Great Britain by Mackays of Chatham plc, Kent

For Isabella

Introduction

What's the toughest thing that you've ever had to endure? Maybe you broke your leg and ended up in hospital, or ran the school cross-country race in the rain? Have you ever been camping in winter? Do you enjoy getting to the top of a hill on a windy day? And have you *ever* gone for longer than a week without anything normal to eat?

If you don't like the idea of being **cold, uncomfortable, wet** or **hungry,** this book may make you shudder. But don't worry. It's much, much safer to read *OUCH!* than to feature in its pages. This book is full of stories about people who have pushed themselves to the very limits of endurance. The kind of people who think of a tent as luxurious accommodation. The kind of people who don't seem happy unless they are doing things like swimming in freezing cold seas, running triathlons, falling off mountains and paddling boats down rivers filled with man-eating crocodiles.

It's also about the (sometimes terrible) things that humans put each other through – and about all the

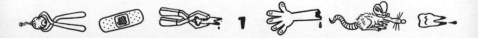

trials of living on an exciting planet, where almost anything can happen.

Whether you are an endurance expert or a luxury-loving layabout, you'll be amazed to see just what we're made of.

How could they?

Do you ever wonder how people could have lived in caves, eaten raw meat or even managed without an indoor loo? What we can put up with depends on what we're used to. And, if it came down to it, you might be able to endure a whole lot more than you think you can!

Everyday hardships for an average ten-year-old	
. . . in the twenty-first century	**. . . in the nineteenth century**
• The central heating stops working in the middle of winter • You can't chat to your friends online because your broadband is down • Your mum doesn't buy your favourite cereal this week • You get soooo much homework and the maths is really tricky • The batteries in your games console run out when you're just about to get to the next level	• The only heating your family has comes from one fire – and it's not in your bedroom • You can't see your friends because they all have consumption (a very serious coughing disease) • It's porridge for breakfast every day – and that's only if you're lucky • You have to work in a factory from dawn to dusk, even on Saturdays • What are batteries?

Some people can't get enough of frightening and dangerous exploits. The reason could be adrenaline – a hormone that surges through your body in times of danger and makes you feel very alert and alive. Being in danger gives you a chance to save your own skin!

Ernie's *Endurance*

On 9 August 1914 a man called Ernest Shackleton embarks from Plymouth on the expedition of a lifetime. Taking some fearless explorers with him, he sets sail south in a ship called the *Endurance*. His plan is to cross the Antarctic via the South Pole, using dog sledges (a trip so dangerous that nobody has even bothered trying before). As you will see, this expedition ends up testing the patience, as well as the physical endurance, of Shackleton and his men.

Trial 1 The first thing Shackleton has to put up with is his ship becoming wedged in ice before reaching land in Antarctica. A frustrating but not impossible situation. OK, the radio isn't working so they can't call for help, but all they have to do is wait until the ice breaks up in the spring. Unfortunately the ice just drags the ship further from where they're trying to go.

Trial 2 After a tough winter spent playing football on a white pitch, the ice doesn't break up as planned. But the ship does, because the ice crushes it. How annoying.

Shackleton's only option is to ask his men (and dogs) to get out, put their stuff in some small boats and walk – pulling the boats behind them. Off they go into biting winds, freezing snow and certain frostbite.

Trial 3 The explorers are now stranded on a raft of ice on a sub-zero sea. They can only hope that floating around will bring them closer to land. No chance. After six months the ice breaks up and they have to get in one of their small boats and row along with frostbitten fingers. At night they camp on an ice floe.

> **Stop!** Let's just have a think about how much cold, wet, scary danger is squashed into that last little sentence alone. Sitting comfortably? On with the story then …

Trial 4 A year and a half after last seeing land, the shattered men finally arrive at a place called Elephant Island. A deserted, cold, lonely bit of the world and not somewhere you'd go for a relaxing holiday, but you can bet they're glad to see it. Shackleton knows there's no chance of being rescued, so he decides to row out from there to a whaling station on the tiny island of

South Georgia with five of the crew. It's a short hop 745 miles away across the Southern Ocean, the most dangerous sea in the world.

Trial 5 The men left behind protect themselves against freezing solid by hiding under their upturned rowing boats. At sea, Shackleton and the others fight to keep their boat from sinking, frantically chipping ice off the deck twenty-four hours a day. Their sleeping bags have turned into blocks of ice, so it isn't as if they have anywhere to cuddle up in comfort anyway.

Trial 6 They finally spot the island. But storms drive them on to rocks and it seems like the end of the road (or sea) for Shackleton.

Trial 7 Miraculously they land safely the next evening. But they soon realize that the whaling station (where there are bound to be good solid whale-hunting boats, toasty fires and warm food) is on the other side of

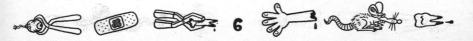

Five essentials for adventures in cold places

Today

- A mobile phone so you can call your mum and the newspapers
- GPS (Global Positioning System) technology so you don't get lost
- High-performance clothes to keep that nasty, cold wind out
- Lightweight waterproof rucksacks filled with NASA-developed food and protein drinks
- An optional film crew to record your achievements for the world to admire (use a camcorder if nobody is brave enough to come with you)

Fifty years ago

- A pencil and paper so you can write a note to whoever finds your body
- A compass and a map (which might be correct, but nobody really knows)
- A warm woolly jumper – well, it's not that warm when it gets wet, and it's a bit itchy, but it's better than nothing
- Heavy canvas rucksacks filled with tins (don't forget the tin opener)
- A diary so your grandchildren can publish your memoirs and make lots of money

the island, over a frozen mountain range. Are you starting to think that someone is playing a bad joke on Shackleton? He must have been wondering too. But, with his last reserves of endurance, he leads his men over the treacherous glaciers to the whaling station. Hooray!

Trial 8 Now all he has to do is go back and rescue the rest of his men from their diet of seaweed and seal bones. Three months later he manages it, and the men go down in history for their magnificent feat of endurance – even if they didn't succeed in crossing the Antarctic.

WOW!

The pole is never a stroll

We might have more modern gizmos and ultra-warm clothes these days, but getting to the poles isn't really that much easier than it was back in Shackleton's day – particularly if you are planning to do it solo. After being the first woman to reach the South Pole on her own, Rosie Stancer wanted to make it a double act by reaching the North Pole in 2007. She struggled across 326 miles of ice – often in zero visibility and temperatures that plummeted to –55 °C. (Much much colder than inside your freezer at home!)

As the ice cracked and shifted around her, Rosie was forced to swim across freezing stretches of water. At one point she even had to retrace her steps after the ice split right open next to her tent, just as she was about to go to sleep! In some of the worst weather ever seen on the Arctic ice cap, she had to abandon her expedition when she was only eighty-nine miles from her goal.

Here's what Rosie says about coping with frostbite:
'Pain was part of my life. But I found I didn't cry
out there. Sometimes I would howl like an animal.
That helped.'

   9

Fearless fact

If you get so wrapped up in these stories that you start dehydrating, remember this ... You can collect rain with a funnel, suck water from the roots and leaves of lots of plants, squeeze liquid from fresh elephant dung, suck the blood and eyes of animals – even get liquid from frogs that store moisture in their skins while they sleep in the mud-baked bottoms of water holes. Or you could just go and get a drink from the tap.

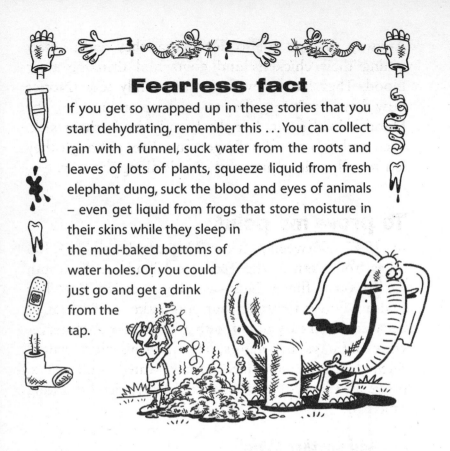

A lot of bottle – but no water!

Lost in the vast Taklamakan desert – in a sunny little spot known as the Sea of Death – explorer Sven Hedin and his men ran out of water. This happened because they hadn't checked that their water bottles were full before leaving the last river. Filling up your water bottle every chance you get is very important in a desert and something that even learner explorers should get right – as Sven was soon to discover.

Anyway, they all got so thirsty that they had to start killing their chickens and goats and drinking their blood. They had a few swigs of brandy too. (Notice how they hadn't forgotten to stock up on brandy.) The blood helped a bit, but the brandy made them sick. Sven and two men finally got out alive, although they left a trail of dead men and camels along the way.

To prove my point . . .

In 1947 Norwegian Thor Heyerdahl sailed 4,300 miles from Peru to the Tuamoto Islands in the South Pacific on a flimsy balsa-wood raft called *Kon-Tiki* (balsa wood is the stuff that you make models out of because it's so easy to cut with a knife). For 101 nerve-wracking days and nights, Thor and his crew drifted through storms and shark-infested waters – all just to prove his theory that settlers could have done it a long time ago.

. . . and another thing!

After more watery adventures, Thor got into ancient reed boats made of papyrus. Everyone said these boats would never make it across the Atlantic because the reeds would get waterlogged after just two weeks in water. Once again, Thor proved them wrong. His first papyrus craft – *Ra* – got within one week's journey of Barbados. His confidence boosted, he tried again with the smaller 12-metre *Ra II*. This time he succeeded in crossing the widest part of the Atlantic from Safi to

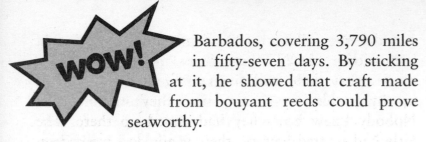

Barbados, covering 3,790 miles in fifty-seven days. By sticking at it, he showed that craft made from bouyant reeds could prove seaworthy.

This is getting out of hand!

Sometimes it's a choice between you or your fingers! After getting deep frozen on one of his daring expeditions to the parky Poles, the explorer Ranulph Fiennes had to cut off his frostbitten fingers to save his own life.

Frostbite is what happens when you get much too cold for much too long. Your fingers, nose, ears and face are the first to suffer because less blood is reaching them. The first warning sign is your skin tingling as it begins to freeze. Unless you can rub the warmth back in, it's downhill from there. Frostbite can spread really quickly and it sometimes ends up with dead bits of you dropping off completely. So, although cutting off your fingers sounds extreme, it could be the only way to save the rest of your hand, arm – or even your life!

Wolf children

Imagine being brought up away from your family – in fact, away from all humans and home comforts

– and living wild. In 1920 Reverend Joseph Singh, a missionary in Northern India, rescued two girls aged about three and five who had been brought up by wolves in a lair since they were babies. Nobody knew how they had ended up there. The girls had matted hair on their heads and walked on all fours.

You might think that life got better for them once they'd been rescued, but you'd be wrong . . . The girls had lived like wolves for so long that they didn't know any other way to act. They tore off their clothes and would only eat raw meat. They slept curled up in a ball, growling and twitching in their sleep, only waking up after the moon rose – when they would howl to be set free. And they'd spent so long on all fours that they couldn't walk upright. The Reverend said their eyes were extra sharp at night and glowed in the dark like a cat's. They could smell a lump of meat right across the yard. Their hearing was very sharp too – but they didn't respond to human voices.

Not long after being rescued, the younger girl got sick and died. The older one did eventually begin to walk, eat normal food and sleep like the other children, but she never really learned to speak and only ever knew about forty words. She died of typhoid when she was still quite young.

Bad food – and not much of it – is just part of the job when you are out exploring. Take German geographer Baron Alexander von Humboldt. On a trip down the Orinoco River in 1800 his food ran out and he ended up munching on ants. So spare him a thought next time you're about to complain about school dinners or that boring sandwich in your packed lunch. Here are some other revolting things that explorers have nibbled on rather than starve to death:

- **Maggots** (quite juicy, but wriggly. Don't bother if you have another choice)
- **Rats** (and other nourishing vermin)
- **Bats** (catch them in caves while they sleep)
- **Bark and leaves** (this doesn't sound too bad, but it's disgusting)

Oh, and explorers sometimes end up drinking their own wee too. Astronauts also do this, but only after it's been purified by special machines.

yuck!

I needed that like a hole in the head

These days we have all kinds of ways to stop things hurting, but in prehistoric times there was much less on

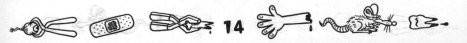

14

offer. One cure that was used for lots of different things – from headaches to bad moods – was cutting a hole in the person's skull. It's called trepanation and the idea was probably to make an escape route for any evil spirits. In some parts of the world it used to be quite common. At one French burial

site that was used around 6500 BC, 40 out of the 120 prehistoric skulls dug up had trepanation holes.

Although you won't find it on offer at your local hospital, there are still people around now who think trepanation will help them feel better. A Dutchman known as 'Doctor' Bart Hughes (although he has never actually completed any medical training) says that it increases 'brain blood volume'.

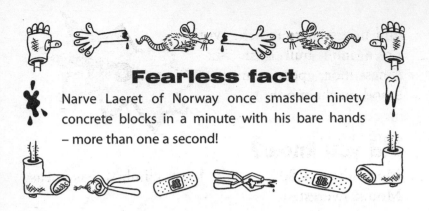

Fearless fact

Narve Laeret of Norway once smashed ninety concrete blocks in a minute with his bare hands – more than one a second!

Now do a lap of honour!

In 2001, while most of us were busy eating, sleeping or watching the telly, twenty-eight-year-old Ellen Macarthur sailed all the way round the world alone in a very small boat. Along the way, she got surrounded by icebergs and ran into waves nearly 19m high – that's like four and a half double-decker buses on top of each other. After getting just twenty minutes' sleep a night for nearly seventy-two days, she sailed past the finish line as a record breaker. As well as doing it faster than anyone else, she was only the second person ever to sail solo

and non-stop round the world on a multi-hull boat. Six times more people have stood on the moon!

Did you know?

More than 1,800 people have climbed easy-peasy Mount Everest.

And that's my last word on the matter . . .

In 1909 Marcel Proust got out his pen and started writing a very long and complicated story called *In Search of Lost Time*. It has seven volumes, some 3,200 pages and more than 2,000 characters (imagine trying to remember all their names!). Proust died in 1922, thirteen years after starting and just before he'd put the finishing touches to the last volumes.

Cook's cabbage cure

Captain James Cook was in charge of some pretty stupendous and punishing sea voyages in the second half of the eighteenth century. Spending a grand sum of six years on the ocean waves to find the Southern Continent – we call it Australia – was just one of his achievements. Like all sailors at the time, he and his crew had to put up with the risk of developing scurvy on the way. This scary disease can be a result of not getting enough vitamin C (just one reason your mum is always telling you to eat more fruit and veg).

If you did get scurvy, your gums would swell up and your teeth would fall out. Then you'd get really weak and finally die. This is obviously not good when you have a hard day's schoolwork ahead of you – and it's

probably even worse when you are on a ship in the middle of an unexplored ocean. Many sailors met their (often toothless) ends before someone worked out the problem. Cook was determined to stop scurvy spoiling his expeditions, so he made all his men eat big plates of pickled cabbage every single day – which tasted really horrible, but was probably slightly better than having scurvy. It was later discovered that limes would do the trick and were much nicer.

Fearless fact

Jackie Bibby, the Texas Snake Man, once held eight live and poisonous rattlesnakes in his mouth by their tails. He also sat in a bath with eighty-one live rattlers and has shared a sleeping bag with 109 of them. And he's only been bitten badly eight times since 1969!

When dentists were a real pain

So you think going to the dentist is tough? Just thank your lucky stars that you live in this century. Not that long ago, your 'operator of the teeth' or

'toothdrawer' could have been a
barber, a watchmaker or even just
a traveller looking to make some easy
money. These operators carried out their
work at markets and fairs – using loud music
to drown out the shouts of their patients. With no
anaesthetics to numb the pain, they had to get rotting
teeth out fast, and there were all kinds of devices to
get the job done, including the terrifying 'key' and the
'pelican'. What with the fear, pain, embarrassment
and the cost, many patients preferred a DIY approach,
using anything from a pair of pliers to
a trusty old door handle and a piece
of string!

The world's hardest job?

Does your mother ever say that you are hard work? Next time she does, tell her this . . . A Russian peasant woman is on record as having an incredible sixty-nine children. Between 1725 and 1765, she gave birth to sixteen sets of twins, seven sets of triplets and four sets of quadruplets. Just imagine the washing up! And how did she ever sort out their socks?

My dream is to stay awake longer than anyone else

In 2007, Tony Wright from Penzance stayed awake for an incredible 266 hours – that's more than eleven days without nodding off. He kept himself going strong with a diet of raw fruit and vegetables and he drank loads of tea. Over the days he did lots of tasks to see how tired he was getting. Strangely he got better at the tasks the longer he went without sleep.

> *Hang on a minute!* Imagine trying to tackle your maths homework when you've been awake for days on end. The chances are that you wouldn't get your best ever mark. So how did Tony manage to do so well?

Well, some scientists believe that the 'low-powered' left side of our brain is holding back the creative right side. But the left side of our brain needs more sleep so, by staying awake for a long time and eating

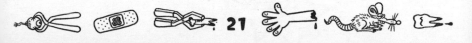

his special food, Tony could actually 'switch off' that side, leaving the right side to storm ahead and do better work!

At the end of his sleepless stint, Tony said that he felt pretty good but admitted that he was looking forward to getting under the duvet.

Up, up and away . . .

Ewa Wisnierska was out paragliding on a sunny day when a freak storm system suddenly sucked her nearly 10,000m up into the sky – higher than the peak of Mount Everest and close to the cruising height of a jumbo jet. Because there's not much oxygen up there, Ewa passed out. She was then whisked around for nearly an hour, covered in ice, through lightning, pounding hail and –40°C temperatures. Amazingly she lived!

WOW!

Row, row, row your boat . . .

Early Viking settlers didn't settle for an easy life. On a mission to find out what lay beyond the seas around Norway, they rowed out into unexplored oceans for weeks on end. They travelled in wooden longboats – big for those days, but tiny compared to those that cross the Channel now. Oarsmen worked in pairs, rowing for long, painful hours before handing over to someone else and going to lie under a scratchy old blanket on the deck for a rest!

In about 1530 some Viking wreckage was found in Iceland. One of the things was an oar with some words carved on it: 'Often I was tired when I pulled you.'

A story about Erik the Red (and a bit puffed out)

Erik was a Viking – Vikings were a tough bunch by any standards, but he was one of the toughest. He led the way in some very arduous longboat voyages . . .

Trip 1 After his family were exiled from Norway when he was a child, Erik and his dad set off across the sea to Iceland. (For you and me, this rowing trip would seem impossible, but for a Viking it was quite a short hop – not even 1,240 miles on the ocean waves.) The

Vikings measured their trips in days, rather than miles, but that didn't make them any shorter.

Trip 2 After growing up big and strong, Erik was banished from Iceland for killing someone. But he'd always longed to explore the world, so he didn't mind too much. His plan was to try to find another land he'd heard about to the west. After a mammoth journey through treacherous seas, icebergs and whales, he succeeded. Erik called his new place Greenland.

Trip 3 Three years later, Erik's banishment was over, so he went back to Iceland to see if anyone else wanted to come and live in Greenland with him. (Greenland wasn't actually very green; its name was a cunning marketing ploy to attract other Vikings bored with the snow.)

Trip 4 Erik's sales technique obviously worked because more than 500 people got into boats and followed him back across the perilous icy seas. Sadly only fourteen of the twenty-five boats made it; the others turned back or were lost at sea.

Like father, like son . . .

Erik the Red had a son – Leif the Lucky. Like his dad, he enjoyed a good long row, so when he heard about new land even further to the west, he got his boat out and set off. Leif eventually discovered Vinland – now called Newfoundland – in America! It's a very long

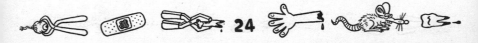

and tricky journey from the coast of Greenland and he was the first known European to visit the Americas. Nobody else managed the journey until Columbus, nearly 500 years later.

I sawed my own hand off

In April 2003 Aron Ralston went into Bluejohn Canyon in Utah to do a bit of climbing. It's frazzlingly hot in Utah, but Aron was having quite a nice time until . . . a 360kg boulder shifted, crushing his hand and pinning him to the canyon wall. Now 360kg is the same weight as a young elephant, so getting it off your hand is no easy matter. For six days, Aron struggled to free himself, getting thirstier and thirstier as his water ran low.

With no rescue teams in sight, Aron realized that unless he could escape, he was facing certain death. There

was only one way out. He angled his arm against a chockstone and broke the ulna and radius bones. Then, using a basic multi-tool, the desperate climber cut off his own right hand, sawing through nerves and muscle and using the tool's pliers on the tougher bits to get the job done as quickly as possible. (Well, you wouldn't want to hang around, would you?)

Once his hand was off, Aron headed home and has since become a bit of a star, appearing on big American television and radio shows and writing a book called *Between a Rock and a Hard Place*. And he's even gone back to mountaineering, becoming the first person ever to climb all of Colorado's mountains over 4,256m high in wintertime.

WOW!

The real Robinson Crusoe

Alexander Selkirk was a Scottish sailor who, from 1704, spent four years alone on an uninhabited island – Juan Fernández. His story was probably the inspiration for the book *Robinson Crusoe* by Daniel Defoe.

Funnily enough, Alex asked to be left on the island – because he was afraid that the ship he was travelling

on was going to sink! But, as he saw the boat sailing away, he realized he'd made a bad decision and chased after it. Unfortunately the captain was a bit fed up with Alex's moaning and sailed off anyway, leaving him shouting on the beach. For a long time he stayed there, scared of everything from sea creatures to strange sounds, becoming lonely and depressed.

Months later he had to move inland when some very noisy sea lions collected on the beach to mate. In one way his life got a bit better because he had new foods to choose from, including wild goats for meat

and milk, turnips, cabbage and pepper berries. Rats were a bit of a problem because they gnawed on his toes at night, but he solved the problem by making friends with some wild cats.

Alex was really clever with the things he'd taken from the ship or found on the island. When his clothes wore out, he made new ones from goatskin using a nail to sew with. (He didn't need shoes because the soles of his feet got so tough!) He built two huts out of trees and used his gun and knife to hunt and clean goats. When his gunpowder started to run out, he had to chase after his food on foot – during one of these hunts he tumbled off a cliff and knocked himself out for about twenty-four hours.

Two ships came and went before Alex finally got off his island prison. Both were Spanish and, because Britain and Spain didn't get on in those days, Alex would have faced a fate worse than death if he'd tried to hitch a lift – so he hid both times. The castaway was finally rescued after four years on 2 February 1709, babbling with joy.

Pardon me, pardon me, pardon me, pardon me . . .

The world record for the longest continuous bout of hiccups goes to Charles Osborne from Iowa in the USA. The hiccups started in 1922 at a rate of forty times a minute, before slowing down to a much more manageable twenty a minute and eventually stopping in February 1990 – a very long sixty-eight years after that first pardon me!

Mum, that shark just bit off my arm . . .

Early one morning in 2003, thirteen-year-old Bethany Hamilton picked up her surfboard and went to Makua Beach in Hawaii to have some fun. She was paddling along in the warm water when a tiger shark – that's one of the big nasty ones with really sharp teeth –

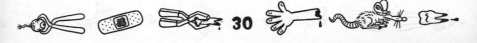

suddenly bit off her left arm, just below the shoulder. Instead of panicking and  drowning, brave Bethany used the only arm she had left to paddle over to her friends for help. Along the way, she shouted out to warn other surfers and swimmers about the shark – and her friends and family say that she never even cried. (Makes all that fuss about stubbing your toe seem a bit embarrassing, doesn't it?)

After such a horrible time, most people would have given up surfing for good, but Bethany was back in the waves on a custom-made board within weeks of her accident, teaching herself to surf with one arm (she says that she has to kick a lot harder now). She started entering competitions again, and although officials offered her extra time to paddle out to sea, Bethany asked to be treated like everyone else. Since then, she has made it to plenty of finals and won three contests. She has also written books, starred in DVDs and even has her own website!

Marco Polo

In the late thirteenth century, Marco Polo, one of the most determined travellers ever, spent twenty-four years finding his way around Asia. On the way he coped with

dry deserts, scary seas, vicious villains, spooky spirits, anti-social animals and much more. There were some good bits too, like staying in the Great Khan's palace, where the walls were covered in gold and silver and the dining hall could seat 6,000 people. When he got back, nobody really believed his stupendous tales. Some of them *were* a bit far-fetched – like the one about birds dropping elephants from great heights. He wrote everything down though, so you could always read his stories yourself and make up your own mind.

Bless you

Probably the longest sneezing bout ever was endured by Donna Griffith. It started in January 1981 and carried on until September 1983, lasting for 978 days, 4,687,514 aaaaah . . . tishoos and goodness knows how many tissues. Poor Donna could only go to sleep when she was exhausted enough to doze off between sneezes.

unlucky!

Freaky food fact

The world record for eating cow brains is held by Takeru Kobayashi who ate nearly eight kilos of them in fifteen minutes. Yum! He also ate fifty-three and a half hotdogs (with buns) in twelve minutes.

yuck!

Bit of a saw spot

Having an operation used to be a real endurance feat. These days, doctors give you an anaesthetic before operating, which means that you don't feel a thing until you wake up. But until about 150 years ago nobody had come up with a really good way of stopping the pain.

  **33**

To be a great surgeon before that, you had to be quick off the mark. The main aim was to get the operation over with before your patient died of shock. (People used to go and watch surgery for fun, so your reputation was at stake if too many of your patients died!)

Langeback, a surgeon in Napoleon's time, claimed that he could 'amputate a shoulder in the time it took to take a pinch of snuff'. (That's smelly stuff to stick up your nose.) But operating could be hard on the surgeons too. Some came out of the operating theatre looking pale and sick. Others were cruel enough to tell their victims – sorry, patients – to be quiet.

One young surgeon who'd always been a bit impatient with his patients changed his tune when he had an operation on his own hand. After it was all over, he promised, 'I never again shall swear at a patient . . .'

Metal munch

For some reason, lots of people have tried to eat metal. Usually they hurt themselves and sometimes they die, but one man who has been munching on metal nearly all his life looks pretty healthy on his strange diet. His name is Michel Lotito, or Monsieur Mangetout – which means Mr Eat-All. (A mangetout is also a small green vegetable, but he doesn't bother with those.) His biggest achievement has been to eat a Cessna 150 light aircraft. He started breaking bits off it in June 1978 and snacked on it a few times a day till he finished the whole thing in 1980. Monsieur Mangetout has also scoffed down:

- **shopping trolleys**
- **television sets**
- **aluminium skis**
- **bicycles – apparently the chain is the tastiest part**
- **knitting needles**
- **plates**
- **coins**
- **glasses and bottles**
- **cutlery**

- **beer cans**
- **bullets**
- **nuts and bolts**
- **razor blades**

Doctors have worked out that part of what Monsieur Mangetout swallows is broken down by very powerful digestive juices, and that the linings of his stomach and intestines are twice as thick as normal – so they can cope with things that would probably kill you or me. But Monsieur Mangetout can't stomach soft food like eggs and bananas – he says they make him feel sick!

weird!

Mini madness

John Evans is a man who likes to balance things on his head – everything from lots of oil drums to milk crates. In one hour, he kept ninety-two people up in the air (not all at the same time!). He sometimes pops a Mini Cooper on his head for fun, and in 2006 he balanced a 3.9-metre-high tower of seven patio tables for ten seconds.

ouch!

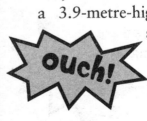

A little on the crunchy side . . .

Fancy an insect for lunch? Maybe not, but in some parts of the world they are a delicacy. People have been eating insects in Japan since ancient times and if you go to a restaurant in Tokyo, you might have the chance to taste some of these treats:

- **Hachi-no-ko** – boiled wasp larvae
- **Zaza-mushi** – aquatic insect larvae
- **Inago** – fried rice-field grasshopper
- **Semi** – fried cicada
- **Sangi** – fried silk-moth pupae

Now doesn't that make your broccoli seem a bit more tempting?

Bee very, very careful

Have you ever been stung by a bee? If so, you might feel a bit sorry for the poor boy in this story. If you haven't, just beeeeeeeeeware . . .

In 1964 a Zimbabwean boy was stung 2,243 times by a gigantic swarm of angry bees. He ran away and tried to hide from them by ducking underwater in a river, but he had to keep popping up for air, where the bees were still waiting. They stung him until his head turned black and swelled up like a football. Amazingly he lived to tell the tale!

Coldest – Vostok at the South Pole. This Russian base is the coldest place on earth. The lowest temperature recorded there was –89.4 °C! To help you imagine how cold that is, water freezes into ice at 0 °C and the temperature in a freezer is about –20 °C. One reason for Vostok's incredible chilliness is that its wind speeds reach 200mph.

Wettest – Cherrapunji, in the Indian state of Meghalaya. 1,290m above sea level, Cherrapunji gets an annual rainfall of over 12m. Once it rained 22.9m in one season!

Driest – The Atacama Desert on the Pacific Coast of Chile. Here, between Arica and Antofagasta, these incredibly dry mountains see an average of less than .01cm of rain per year. This area often goes without any rainfall at all for years on end.

Hottest – El Azizia in Libya, on the northern part of the African continent. On 13 September 1922, the mercury hit a horribly hot 57.8 °C. This wasn't the temperature on the ground, which can reach 66 °C, but the air temperature at 1.6m above the ground, where it's cooler.

Forty degrees below zero

About one hundred years ago, Antarctica was an almost unexplored white patch on the map of the world. Lots of eager adventurers tried to travel there, and this is the story of the most famous – Captain Robert Falcon Scott. Scott had already been on one successful expedition to Antarctica when in 1910 he decided to go back and be the first to get all the way to the South Pole.

Soon after Scott's party had set off for the Pole on 24 October 1911, their motor sledges broke down. In the freezing weather every day became a battle to survive. The ponies had to be shot about 250 miles out. After that the dog teams were sent back. By New Year's Eve, seven men had also been packed off back to base.

The rest of the men – Scott, Lawrence Oates, Edger Evans and two others – struggled on through blizzards and gales. When they got to the South Pole on 18 January 1912 they found that a Norwegian team led by Roald Amundsen had beaten them there by about a month. After eighty-one days of suffering, they were crushed.

The weather on the way back was horrendous and they soon started running out of food and fuel. Evans died on 17 February. A month later, Oates crawled out of the tent and disappeared into the snow – a sad way to celebrate his thirty-second birthday. His brave last words have gone down in history: 'I am just going outside and may be some time . . .'

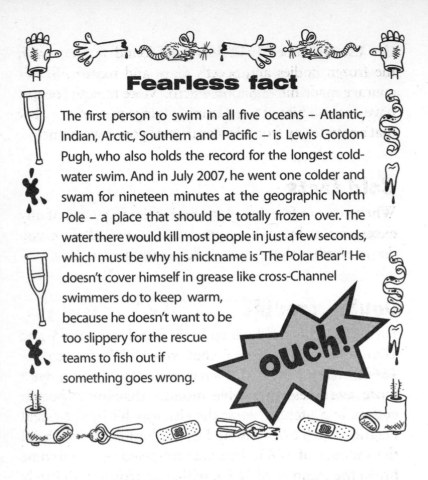

Fearless fact

The first person to swim in all five oceans – Atlantic, Indian, Arctic, Southern and Pacific – is Lewis Gordon Pugh, who also holds the record for the longest cold-water swim. And in July 2007, he went one colder and swam for nineteen minutes at the geographic North Pole – a place that should be totally frozen over. The water there would kill most people in just a few seconds, which must be why his nickname is 'The Polar Bear'! He doesn't cover himself in grease like cross-Channel swimmers do to keep warm, because he doesn't want to be too slippery for the rescue teams to fish out if something goes wrong.

OUCH!

The three survivors struggled on for around ten miles before a blizzard trapped them in their tents. They were just eleven miles away from a food depot – but the whirling snow made it impossible for them to get there. Scott took out his journal and wrote his last letter to his wife. His fingers almost paralysed by the brutal cold, he wrote that he was barely alive, with little food and fuel left. He and his team died soon after of cold and starvation.

On 12 November 1912 searchers found the tent with the frozen bodies and Scott's diary and records. Scott's courage made him a national hero. More recently, people have accused him of not planning things properly . . . but that's easy to say from the comfort of your own home!

Cold facts

When you are freezing, your body tries to get rid of any excess water by making you want to wee. Before you do, remember that exposed flesh can freeze!

Double trouble

If you had the bad luck to be in London in 1665 and 1666, the chances were that you didn't live to see 1667. Anyone who did survive had to put up with more awfulness in twelve months than most people endure in a lifetime. First the city was hit by the Great Plague, which exterminated whole families throughout the summer of 1665. This was followed by a fearsome fire in the summer of 1666, which destroyed the closely packed houses – and finally put an end to your chances of dying from the Great Plague.

When the putrid plague struck London in 1665, nobody knew how long it was going to go on for, or how it passed from one person to another. For a long time rats got the blame, but scientists have recently discovered that it could have been a virus. Mothers,

fathers, brothers and sisters died within days of each other. Everyone breathed in a stink of death, illness, unwashed bodies, streets full of sewage – and the open pits that were dug to fling dead bodies into. There was one called the Great Pit at Aldgate and another at Finsbury Fields. (And there are lots of less well-known plague pits under everyday houses in London today!)

As more and more people became infected, things just got worse. If anyone showed signs of having the plague, they and the rest of their family would be locked inside their house to die one by one. The door was painted with a red cross and the words: 'Lord have mercy on us.' At night, carts came around, with a shout of 'Bring out your dead'. The corpses were brought out, put in a cart and taken away to the pits.

The agonizing symptoms of the Great Plague:

- **a ring-shaped rash (the one children sing about in 'Ring-a-ring of Roses')**
- **skin turning black in patches**
- **glands swelling up to the size of apples**
- **compulsive vomiting**
- **swollen tongue**
- **splitting headaches**
- **death**

So you're feeling a bit poorly? Here are some things that you could catch off your friends . . .

. . . these days

- Nits – your mum or dad can get rid of them with some smelly shampoo and a metal comb
- The common cold – there's no cure for this, but it'll get better on its own in a few days
- Chickenpox – don't scratch and you'll be fine in a while
- A stomach bug – this can be quite nasty but it's not likely to be serious. Just keep sipping water and stay off the pizza

These days, doctors are really very clued up and can cure many problems. We also know a lot more about illness than our ancestors did.

. . . in the old days

- All over lice – your parents have them too, so you'll just have to put up with the never-ending itching and bleeding
- The bubonic plague – there's no cure for this either. You and your family are likely to be dead in a few days
- Smallpox – even if you survive you'll be horribly scarred for life
- Cholera – a pretty horrible disease where you die of diarrhoea . . . In the 1850s, cholera often came free with your drinking water

In those days, doctors were pretty clueless, so you just had to put up with being ill until you got better or died.

Ultra-marathon man

Running a marathon (more than twenty-six miles) is a mega task, and if you ever finish one you should be very proud of yourself. But, for some runners, anything less than fifty miles is a baby step. They just hit their stride and keep on going. One ultra-marathon man – Yiannis Kouros – has set records almost beyond belief. In 1997 he ran 186 miles in twenty-four hours. That's like doing seven marathons one after the other! He has also managed to run more than one hundred miles a day, for six days straight. Can you imagine the state of his trainers?

So lightning never strikes twice?

Only one in ten people who are struck by lightning die – the other nine live to tell the tale. The most long-suffering lightning victim was park ranger Roy Sullivan – aka the 'human lightning conductor'. Roy got hit a very unlucky seven times between 1942 and 1977. Even though he survived all seven strikes, he did suffer some serious side effects – like having his hair set alight, losing his big toenail and eyebrows and getting some very nasty injuries to his arms, legs, chest and stomach.

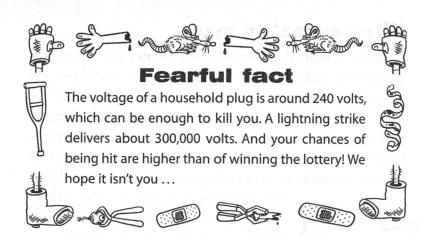

Fearful fact

The voltage of a household plug is around 240 volts, which can be enough to kill you. A lightning strike delivers about 300,000 volts. And your chances of being hit are higher than of winning the lottery! We hope it isn't you ...

Come on in - the water's lovely

Next time you're at the beach, dipping your toes in the sea and feeling a bit shivery, just imagine setting off on a very long, very cold swim out to the horizon and beyond. Marathon swimming is an endurance sport that pits your body against everything that the sea has to throw at it – including very big waves, storms, swarms of jellyfish, sharks, oil slicks and hypothermia . . .

For hardy marathon swimmers, dressing for the occasion just means putting on a well-fitting pair of bathers and a big tub of body grease. Wetsuits are for sissies. In fact, American swimmer Ted Erikson – the second person to cross the English Channel both ways in 1965 – said that wearing a wetsuit in a marathon swim is like 'completing the Tour de France on a moped'.

On 7 April 2007 a man called Martin Strel swam the whole length of the Amazon River in sixty-six days. He covered a colossal 3,274 miles – further than the width of the Atlantic Ocean. As well as swimming a very long way, he also had to put up with swarms of insects and other nasty biting creatures. Escort boats poured blood into the river to distract meat-eating fish, like piranhas and sharks, away from him. Near the end of his swim, he came face-to-face with the Pororoca – a tidal bore (very big wave) about four metres high.

Take it to the limit

Does the human body have limits? Well, maybe it still does today, but who knows how far people could go in the future? New records of sporting endurance are being set all the time. Triathlons encourage athletes to push their bodies further and further. And even though running a mile in four minutes was once thought impossible (in 1954 Roger Bannister was considered almost superhuman for achieving it), today the four-minute mile is a regular event in senior schools!

Every breath you take . . .

Free diving is a risky race to go further and further underwater on a single breath of air. After holding his breath for an incredible nine minutes and four

seconds on 13 December 2006, Herbert Nitsch of Austria shattered the record held by French free diver Loïc Leferme. Loïc died soon after, training to win the record back.

Some pretty horrible feats

Watch a ballerina floating elegantly across the stage and it's difficult to imagine how much she has had to put up with behind the scenes. Dancers in training often keep going until their feet are inflamed and sore, and they often have corns growing between their toes due to the pressure placed on their bones. Talk about suffering for your art!

yuck!

Teenage traveller

Fifteen-year-old Jordan Maguire from Scotland became the youngest boy to walk to the North Pole in April 2006. He completed his journey in ten days, after travelling on foot from North Russia to the Arctic, making his incredible feat look almost easy.

WOW!

Are we nearly there yet . . . ?

. . . in the old days

- It took days on end to get from Scotland to London on a stagecoach – you felt every pothole like a blow, it cost a lot extra to sit inside in the warmth and highway robbers lurked round every corner waiting to take your mum's jewels on pain of death.

- When convicts were packed off to Australia by boat in the 1800s they spent eight months getting there, many suffering terrible seasickness, malaria and typhoid all the way.

- During the Irish Potato Famine of 1846, starving men, women and children were crammed into rat-infested boats going to America. The journey took up to three months and the boats became known as coffin ships because so many died on board.

. . . these days

- The train trip from Edinburgh to London takes around five hours now, the seats are quite comfy, there's a loo down the corridor and you can get a sandwich and drink whenever you want.

- A plane journey to Australia is probably the longest trip you're likely to make these days – twenty-four hours on board an aircraft is fairly hard going, but at least there's usually a good film to watch, and you get your own seat.

- Boarding an ocean liner to the States could well be one of the most glamorous modern-day journeys. It might take a few weeks, but with on-board cinemas and pools, you'll have a life of luxury all the way.

Are you listening at the back?

On 1 April 1988 in New York, Dr Donald Thomas started an after-dinner speech about Vegetarian Athletic Nutrition. (I expect you are asleep already, so take pity on the poor guests.) The doctor's speech lasted an unspeakable thirty-two hours and twenty-five minutes. Or was that an after-breakfast speech?

Upside-down water torture

Harry Houdini was one of the first to wow the world with his feats of daring and endurance. Way back in 1913, his star turn was the Upside-down Water Torture Cell. His ankles were fixed into a brace and he was put underwater, upside down and locked in place in full view of the audience. From this position he freed himself and escaped from the water cell.

   **49**

Fearless fact

Ken Edwards from Derbyshire, England, once ate thirty-six cockroaches in one sitting. He said: 'It's like having an anaesthetic at the back of the throat.' Well, maybe it isn't as bad as it sounds, then, Ken! By the way, cockroaches are very good at endurance too – although the theory that they are the only living creatures capable of surviving a nuclear attack isn't true.

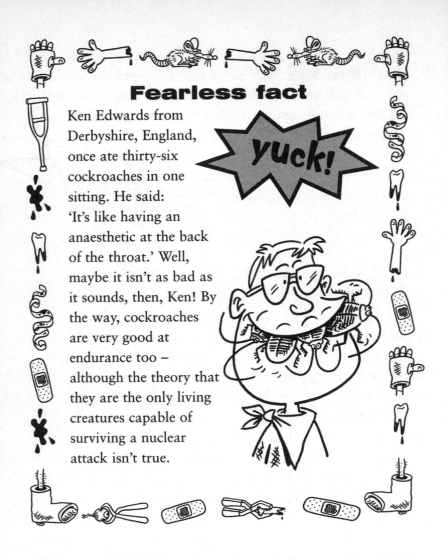

Nearly finished!

Antonio Gaudi, a famous Catalan architect, spent years on his masterpiece – the Sagrada Familia in Barcelona. This giant church, which he started in 1882, is still

being worked on today. Gaudi put everything he had into the building. As he got older, he practically lived on site and ended up looking like a tramp. He died in 1926 after falling under a tram – reportedly while stepping backwards into the road to admire his work. Because he looked so scruffy, cab drivers refused to take him to hospital.

unlucky!

It's tough at the top – and even tougher at the bottom

The story of Joe Simpson, Simon Yates and their accident on Siula Grande in the Andes is truly harrowing. It all started off as an innocent day's mountain-climbing, but things soon took a turn for the worse.

The broken leg First of all, Joe broke his leg by smashing into the ice when his hold slipped on a tricky cliff. The blow made him slide head first off the mountain. He came to a stop hanging from his rope, upside down and in agony from his twisted, crushed leg.

The only way down Simon came to help and, miraculously, they both got back to safer ground. The only way down the next bit was for Simon to lower Joe on a long rope – his bad leg bashing into the side of the mountain every few seconds.

The big fall They had to get down nearly a thousand metres a bit at a time, but with frostbitten fingers, Simon was finding it harder and harder to lower Joe. Then the slope turned into a drop and Joe ended up hanging in space on his rope (again) – with at least thirty metres below him. There was no way up or down.

The hard decision Simon did his best to pull Joe back up. But the rope wouldn't budge! Simon had to make a really hard decision: his climbing partner was dangling in thin air, unlikely to come back up alive, and his weight would soon pull Simon to almost certain death too. After what seemed like a lifetime, with his frozen fingers rubbed raw from Joe's weight, Simon cut the rope.

The unlucky break Joe went speeding downwards through thin air, thinking that he was bound to die. He landed on an ice ledge – stunned, numb, sick and with all the breath knocked out of him. But he was alive.

Put yourself in Joe's place for a minute . . .
Imagine you have fallen off a mountain, dangled on a rope and then suddenly crashed down on to hard ice. Your leg is useless and agonizingly painful. It's almost totally dark and bitterly cold, and there is an unknown drop on either side of you. What would you do?

Joe didn't have many choices. He decided to use the rest of the rope to lower himself down into the depths below. Miraculously, he reached an ice floor. And, when dawn arrived, he was able to climb out to the side of the mountain.

The long cold walk But Joe wasn't quite home and dry yet – he still had to get off the mountain and cross a very big rocky field with no water or food and a badly broken leg. He forced himself on by chanting, 'Move, stop dozing, move!'

Only an incredible amount of determination got Joe Simpson through his ordeal. Simon Yates survived as well, after a stressful time getting down the mountain.

Let's go round again . . .

Fifteen rounds of getting punched on the nose in one of today's professional boxing matches may seem like a bit of an endurance test for anyone, but it's not as tough as it once was. In fact, with matches over in less than an hour, today's boxers have it pretty easy. A hundred years ago (when nobody had a telly to go home to) some boxers kept hitting each other for hours on end.

One of the most famous long fights took place on 6 April 1893 in New Orleans. For a prize of $2,500 – a

fortune in those days – Andy Bowen and Jack Burke set out to 'fight to the finish'. After seven hours and nineteen minutes, and a massive 110 rounds, the boxers collapsed in a heap. The match was declared 'no contest' – a verdict that was later changed to a draw.

Holdouts

For many years after the Second World War had ended, Japanese soldiers were still living and fighting in remote parts of the jungle – not realizing that the war was over. These groups were called holdouts. Some were discovered in just a few months, others stayed hidden for decades, living on beetles, berries and rainwater, and dying out slowly through disease, wounds or accidents. One of the most famous survivors of a holdout was Hiroo Onada, who finally came out into a very changed world in 1974.

   **54**

Sea you later . . .

In 1982 Steven Callahan set sail from the Canary Islands on a small boat he built himself. Just six days into the trip, disaster struck. Steven's boat sank and he was left floating around the ocean on a 1.5m inflatable life raft.

You *can* try this at home . . .

To get an idea of how big Steven Callahan's raft was, ask four of your friends to lie down on the floor head to toe, making a square. Then sit down in the middle of the square. You'll see that getting comfy is pretty tricky. Now, half close your eyes and imagine that outside your friends all you can see are miles and miles of deep, deep, deep ocean – and lots of hungry sharks.

Things weren't too bad on the raft to start with: Steven had 1.4kg of food – about the same weight as twenty sausages – and 4.5l of fresh water (plus about a billion gallons of salty seawater). Plenty to keep the average twelve-year-old fed and watered for about . . . a day and a half.

The really stinking bit of Steven's story is that he didn't get rescued until seventy-six days later. That's nearly eleven weeks alone at sea – and with nobody to talk to it must have seemed even longer. Exposed to the elements and with no help in sight, poor Steven got very badly sunburned, lost masses of weight and had to keep fighting off sharks (he probably got less appetizing as he got bonier). Every time a ship passed in the distance he became hopeful, but they all sailed past without noticing the tiny speck waving frantically at them. By the time Steven was finally picked up, he had travelled nearly 1,900 miles – like going halfway from London to Hong Kong.

Steven wouldn't have stayed alive without . . .

- **His solar still** – which gets fresh drinking water out of saltwater.
- **The spear** he made for fighting off sharks and catching fish. (He had to eat the fish raw, but they were very fresh!)
- **A strong will** – to keep hoping, catching fish and finding ways to occupy his mind.

- **Quick thinking** – even when his raft sprung a leak, Steven kept it afloat by managing the leak for thirty-three more days until he was rescued.

Drowned alive

David Blaine is an American who likes to prove just how much the human body can endure. In 2006 he attempted a big publicity stunt – a week underwater connected to air only by a breathing tube, followed by a target of holding his breath underwater for nine long minutes. He managed seven minutes and eight seconds, then blacked out. Coming back out into fresh air, he was devastated by the effects of a week underwater and his failed record attempt.

Before that he had also . . .

- Spent nearly sixty-two hours in a box of ice in Times Square, New York. Air and water came in through one tube – and there was another tube for liquid on its way out!
- Stood on a pillar 27m high and 56cm wide for more than thirty-four hours.
- Spent seven days buried inside a glass coffin at the bottom of an open water-filled pit in front of a building in New York City.
- Fasted for forty-four days inside a see-through case hanging above the ground by Tower Bridge in London. (At one point, a remote-controlled helicopter flew a burger up to make his mouth water.)

He came out 24.5kg lighter and was sent straight to hospital.

Spaced out

It's quite difficult to know what happens to the human body in the vacuum of space – because nobody really wants to pop outside the spaceship without their special suit on. There are stories of bodies exploding and blood boiling, but NASA doesn't seem to think this is very likely. They probably know better than anyone, because when they were doing some tests in a near vacuum, the astronaut's spacesuit leaked. He didn't burst – they think that was because human skin is quite strong. He stayed conscious for about fourteen seconds and could remember the water on his tongue starting to boil before he blacked out (he did survive though). That was back in 1965. Strangely enough, nobody has volunteered to repeat the experiment since.

We're a real bunch of softies

People were so much tougher during what's called the hunter-gatherer age (that's when everyone had to pick or catch their own food). All that hunting and foraging was much, much harder than popping down to the supermarket, and it wasn't unusual for

   **58**

people to do up to ten hours of walking and running every day – just to survive. Nowadays, well-trained athletes preparing for extreme endurance events manage between just 20% and 60% of this.

Today, many of us work in offices (and schools). And sitting at a desk all day doesn't give you any exercise at all. Because of this, we need to do lots of other kinds of activities to keep fit – from long walks to early mornings at the gym. But some people really do take things to extremes . . .

Tough things happen in threes

A triathlon is an athletic event where you swim, cycle and run in three long stretches. It's one of the hardest types of exercise you can imagine. You have to learn to race each stage so that, at the end of each gruelling test, you have enough energy left to change your clothes and get on with the next one. One of the hardest triathlons is the Hawaii Ironman World Championship, which

is famous for being ultra-long and ultra-exhausting. If you're thinking of joining in, this is what you can expect . . .

- **For starters . . .** take a 2.4-mile ocean swim in Kailua-Kona Bay
- **The main course . . .** cycle more than a hundred miles over Hawaii's lava desert, where temperatures often reach over 40 °C and crosswinds can blow at 56mph
- **To finish . . .** a light marathon run (26 miles) along the coast of the Big Island

---

Or why not try to escape from Alcatraz?

Held in San Francisco, this race begins with a 1.5-mile swim in icy-cold waters from the famous Alcatraz prison island to the shore. This is followed by an eighteen-mile bicycle ride and a very hilly eight-mile run, which includes the punishing 'Sand Ladder' – a 400-step staircase climb up a beachside cliff.

A grave mistake

Imagine being in a coffin under the ground with everyone thinking you are dead. Nobody would be buried alive accidentally today, but it did happen in the

past. Without all the fancy machines we have now to measure brain activity and other signs of life, there was no sure-fire way to tell whether someone was really and truly gone – especially if they were in a coma. So sometimes a patient opened his eyes and gave everyone a shock!

Getting buried too soon was more likely to happen during busy times – like plagues – when doctors were overworked and didn't want to get too close to the body in case they caught the disease. Some people were so worried about being buried alive that they made sure they could get out again. One escape route was to have a bell put above your grave with a string attached, which fed through to the inside of the coffin,

so that the victim could give it a tug if they woke up. Other 'safety coffins' had flags. You just had to hope that people liked you enough to visit your grave and hear your call for help!

A woman was pronounced dead and buried. A few hours later she was dug up by grave robbers who wanted to steal her jewellery. (So much for resting in peace!) When they opened her casket, the woman sighed and woke up. The robbers ran off, the woman went home, gave her husband a bit of a shock and ended up outliving him!

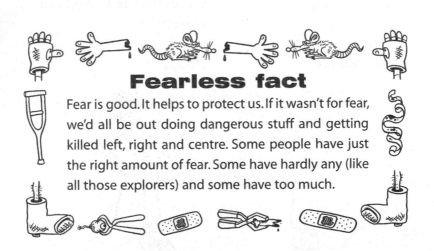

Fearless fact

Fear is good. It helps to protect us. If it wasn't for fear, we'd all be out doing dangerous stuff and getting killed left, right and centre. Some people have just the right amount of fear. Some have hardly any (like all those explorers) and some have too much.

Terrified of peanut butter?

For some people, just leaving the house is an endurance test. For others, it's seeing a spider running up the wall. If you have panophobia – which means fear of absolutely everything – everyday life can be more of a trial than climbing Mount Everest. Here are some of the strangest phobias.

Phobia	Fear of
Ablutophobia	washing or bathing
Arachibutyrophobia	peanut butter sticking to the roof of your mouth
Blennophobia	slime
Bogyphobia	the bogeyman
Clinophobia	going to bed
Genuphobia	knees
Levophobia	things on the left side of your body
Linonophobia	string
Nephophobia	clouds

Phobia	Fear of
Ostraconophobia	shellfish
Papyrophobia	paper
Peladophobia	bald people
Phobophobia	fear
Pogonophobia	beards
Scolionophobia	school – also known as didaskaleinophobia
Xanthophobia	the colour yellow

weird!

Rat for tea?

How hungry would you have to be to eat a rat? When German troops surrounded the Russian city of St Petersburg – Leningrad – in 1941, they planned on starving the locals out. Very little food or other supplies got in, and with 2 million mouths to feed, hundreds of thousands of people died of starvation, disease and exposure. After many long, cold and extremely hungry months, any food had run out or gone off – and all but the most cherished of pets had already been eaten. People had no energy, little hair and few teeth left. Those with enough strength fought over anything they could find to eat – including rats in the streets. The siege went on for 872 long days.

Potato panic

In the nineteenth century, most people in Ireland had little to eat apart from potatoes. That was bad enough when the harvest was good, so imagine the horror when the potato crops failed. This happened in 1846 when a potato disease called the blight struck. It spread fifty miles a week across the countryside, destroying nearly every potato in Ireland. There were only enough potatoes to feed everyone for a single month. That meant eleven further months without food.

Panic swept the country. The very old and young were the first to get ill from malnutrition. Nobody knows how many died, but probably around one million people starved to death from 1846 to 1849. Those still alive were desperate for a way out. Some landlords sent poor families overseas to British North America with phoney promises of money, food and clothing. Half-naked people were jammed into overcrowded, poorly built British sailing ships. So many people died on board that these rat-riddled vessels became known as coffin ships.

The first coffin ships headed for Quebec in Canada. The 3,000-mile journey could take anything from forty days to three months. The conditions on board were terrible, and typhus and other fevers spread like wildfire. In the spring of 1847, shipload after shipload of seriously ill people arrived. With only 150 beds, the small medical area in Quebec just couldn't cope.

And that's when the boats started queuing. By June, forty ships holding 14,000 Irish immigrants waited in

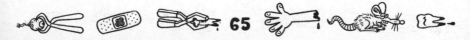

a line two miles long down the St Lawrence River. A month later, the line of ships had grown several miles long.

Then the doctors started catching typhus from the passengers – so they stopped people landing. Forced to wait day after day on board, even those who had arrived healthy got ill. With so many dying, hundreds of bodies were simply dumped overboard into the water.

Golden lilies

Until it was banned in 1919, most Chinese families who wanted their daughters to get on in life (as in marry a rich, successful man rather than run a multi-national company) had the girls' feet bound into what were called 'golden lilies'. This meant wrapping the tiny tootsies tightly to stop them from growing – as smaller feet were thought more attractive.

At around the age of six, the girls' toes were curled under their feet and wrapped in bandages. The girls

were then made to walk until their bones broke. Every day the bandages were taken off and new ones put on. By the time the girls were old enough to get married, their feet were small – but they were also deformed and basically useless. A single step was an ordeal, but many of these women had to run their homes and bring up their children. (And if they had daughters the whole thing started all over again.)

ouch!

You're collared!

The collar was one of the nasty punishments used in London's Clink prison. It was a horribly heavy and tight metal ring, lined with lead and sharp spikes, which was put around the poor prisoner's neck. As well as suffering under such a torturous weight, they couldn't lie down because the spikes stuck in their skin – and then they got lead poisoning through the cuts and usually died soon after.

It's not really the bullets that bother me . . .

As well as having to put up with bullets, bombs and all that other deadly stuff, soldiers have also had some really bothersome day-to-day dilemmas to cope with – especially those on the front line. Some soldiers have said that these everyday aggravations can be worse than the worry of being hurt or killed . . .

- **Rats**
- **Horrible toilets (or no toilets)**
- **No baths**
- **Living with other people with smelly socks**
- **Swarms of flies and other insects**
- **Missing your home and family**
- **Endless days of boredom**
- **Uncomfortable clothes and boots**
- **Being ordered around**
- **Really gruesome food**
- **Trench foot**

My toes are coming off

Soldiers on the Western Front in the First World War lived in waterlogged trenches and stood up to their knees in mud for hours on end. That's bad enough for starters, but it also meant that most of them suffered from trench foot – a truly horrible condition caused by damp feet. It starts off as blisters and very quickly leads to open sores, gangrene and amputation. To fight it off, you have to change your socks all the time.

British soldiers in the trenches in the First World War had to have three pairs of socks with them and were under orders to dry their feet and change their socks at least twice a day. They were also told to cover their feet with grease made of whale oil. A battalion at the front probably used about ten gallons of whale oil every day.

Burning issues

In the Middle Ages, lots of people were burned at the stake – particularly for going to the wrong kind of church. Many people chose to endure this horrible slow death rather than change their religion. If an executioner was feeling kind (or was bribed), he would put gunpowder in with the wood to speed things up.

Some really bad punishments

Today

- Being grounded
- Having your iPod confiscated
- Pocket money stoppages
- No TV for a week
- Being sent to the head teacher
- Losing your playtime
- Having to help with the washing up
- Detention after school

These days, painful punishments are definitely no go, and you have to be really bad to get locked up before you reach sixteen.

In the past

- Being stretched on a rack
- Being dunked in the village pond
- Being burned at the stake
- Having veg thrown at you in the stocks
- Being locked up for years on end
- Being banished from your home – forever
- Having your head chopped off

Being young wasn't an excuse for anything until quite recently. Joan of Arc was only sixteen when she was burned at the stake!

Trial by fire

Right up until the sixteenth century, before judges and juries were around, there were all kinds of odd ways to decide who was guilty – none of them fair and most of them extremely painful. Trials by Ordeal were particularly hard to endure. In a Trial by Fire, you

had to walk a certain distance – usually three metres – holding a red-hot iron. If your burns had got better after three days, you were innocent. If your wounds hadn't healed, you would be sent away or executed.

Tough as new boots

Soldiers' boots have always given them blisters, which is the last thing you want when you have a mammoth march or fearsome fight ahead of you. In the two World Wars, soldiers discovered a great way to soften their boots up. They did a wee in them and then left them to stand overnight. Well, their feet probably smelt so bad anyway . . .

Napoleon's long, cold march

Napoleon was a military man with some very big ideas. As he got more powerful, he put his troops through all kinds of horrible things. In fact, although the history books call him brilliant, being a soldier in Napoleon's army was probably a pain from beginning to end. One of his least popular ideas (especially with the 600,000 men who had to do it) was conquering Moscow in 1812. For his soldiers, it was a mission that would end up with most of them dying.

Frustrating The march towards Moscow was bad enough, as the Russian army had headed back to

their capital city stripping and burning all the shelter and supplies on their way. Napoleon had planned to use these things to keep his soldiers going, so this wasn't great news – but things were set to get a whole lot worse.

Boring When Napoleon arrived in Moscow, the Russians promptly burned the city down. Now it wasn't even worth conquering! After a few months spent twiddling their thumbs, Napoleon's army couldn't think what to do, so they gave up. As the freezing Russian winter started, they headed home across the frozen wasteland. And that's when it all went rapidly downhill.

Freezing The men fought their way through whirlwinds of snow and sleet. Their clothes were frozen stiff on their bodies and icicles dangled from their hair and beards. There was nothing to eat except scraps of boiled horsemeat, a few potatoes or rye – and lighting a fire to cook anything was almost impossible. Men killed each other for a mouthful of food.

Dying Every day hundreds of Napoleon's men lay down in the snow to die. Their bodies were soon covered by whirling white flakes. By the time Napoleon arrived back in Paris, only 20,000 soldiers were still alive; 580,000 had been lost along the way.

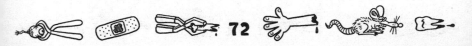

Marathon monks

A group of Buddhist monks push the limits of human endurance to be made saints. They run one hundred consecutive days of marathons (26.2 miles), beginning at half past one in the morning. And they run in a white robe and sandals. (Who needs high-performance trainers?)

Mind over matter?

In India there are people called yogis who claim to live without the bare necessities of food and water. One of these – Giri Bala – says that she hasn't had a bite to eat or a sip of water for over fifty-six years. 'From the age of twelve years four months down to my present age of sixty-eight, I have not eaten food or taken liquids ... nourishment is derived from the finer energies of the air and sunlight, and from the cosmic power that

recharges your body . . .' (Paramahansa Yogananda: *Autobiography of a Yogi*). If this was true it would be a truly science-defying feat of endurance!

Captive

Being held hostage is one of the hardest things to endure because you have no choice in the matter – and no idea whether you will get out alive or end up dead. One of the most famous hostages ever is John McCarthy, who was kept captive by a militant group for 1,943 days . . . While locked up, he had to cope with loneliness, boredom, beatings, having no light and not knowing whether he would be released or executed. He says that his strength came from the people who were kept hostage with him.

Stone me!

Stonehenge was built by some very determined workers. Started in the Stone Age, it was only finished during the Bronze Age more than 3,000 years later (by different people of course!). The smaller stones, which weigh about four tonnes each, came from the wild western parts of Wales. With no lorries and no M4 to get them from one place to another, they had to be dragged over the ground – and the most likely route was about 236 miles long!

The bigger stones were only moved about twelve miles, but they weigh up to 50 tonnes each – the same as an aeroplane. It probably took years to get each one into position. So why all the effort? Nobody knows for sure, but it's possible that the whole operation was part of worshipping a sun god.

In a tight spot

Over the centuries, women (and men) have worn all kinds of corsets under their clothes. These unforgiving undergarments were often made even more painful with whalebone and metal rods, and laced up very tightly to make it look like you had a tiny waist. The problem was that they stopped you breathing properly, which often led to fainting at the drop of a hat. Corsets also made eating very difficult and changed the shape of your back, rib cage and all your squishy organs!

These are just some of the other silly things that people have put up with putting on, just to be fashionable . . .

- Enormously heavy horsehair wigs (which mice would sometimes nest in between styling sessions). Some very fashionable women went one further and had mini birdcages – complete with birds – built into their hairstyles!
- Scratchy tight neck ruffs
- White face powder made with very poisonous lead, which could burn your face and made you ill. Elizabethan women added some colour to their white cheeks by piling on pretty pink rouge . . . with even more lead in it!

- Massive decorated hats that weighed more than your average school rucksack
- High heels that twist ankles and bring you crashing to the floor
- Bustles and layers of enormous petticoats that stopped you getting through doors
- Very tight jeans
- Long false nails that make it impossible to do anything useful

   **76**

Spill the beans – or else

Torture has always been used to get people to tell tales and change their minds about things. It still goes on in some places today, but in the Middle Ages it was the answer to almost any problem anywhere.

The gadgets used to torture people were called things like toe wedge, tongue slicer, copper boot, thumbscrew, foot press, head crusher, whirligig, heretic's spike and other more unmentionable names. We won't go into too many details about what these horrible things did because you might be sick.

A tortured tale

In Britain, it was torture to live during Tudor times. Henry VIII was a great fan of hurting people to get them to say what he wanted them to. Edward and Mary toned things down a bit, but Henry's daughter Elizabeth I really stepped up the pace. While she was Queen there was more torture going on than in any other time in history. People caught stealing had their right hand cut off, eyes were plucked out with hot pincers and fingers were torn off.

Elizabeth thought that treason (saying bad things about, or plotting against, the Queen) was just dreadful, and it was the accusation behind most top torture sessions. She didn't like the idea of poisoning much either and the poisoner's punishment was being boiled to death.

High art

Painting the ceiling of the Sistine Chapel was the achievement of a lifetime for Michelangelo, but he went through a lot to get it all finished. To get it right, he had to lie on his back for four years – 23m off the ground!

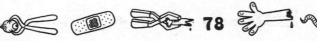 

Now hair's a strange fact

In the past, some monks wore hair shirts when they felt that they had broken their vows. As well as being very itchy, the shirts were often full of lice that bit their skin, making things even worse.

Mad as a snake

Scientists have gone through all kinds of horrible things in the name of progress. From cures for heart disease to space travel, the people who tried things out first were among the bravest of them all. Many – like Marie Curie – died because of their experiments. Some just got painful results.

Take Dr F. Eigenberger, who spent the 1920s taking snake poison to see what would happen. In one experiment, he injected himself with diluted green mamba venom, and then sat back to observe the results. His eyes got sore and his face got numb, he couldn't feel his fingers and toes and it was hard to breathe. Good job he didn't use the full-strength version!

Other adventurous scientists actually died because of their experiments. Marie Curie was a physicist whose research into radioactivity saved lots of lives but

almost certainly ended up killing her. Penniless and living in Paris in the 1890s, she worked every day until dawn in her tiny room – eating almost nothing except bread and butter. With her husband, Pierre Curie, she made two very important discoveries – polonium and radium – both radioactive. Even having two daughters didn't distract Marie from her research and, after her husband was killed in an accident in 1906, she stopped at nothing to finish the work they'd started together. With almost superhuman energy, she built a priceless stockpile of radioactive material, which could be used to treat illness. And when the First World War broke out she saw how X-rays could help find bullets in the wounded, so she invented X-ray vans and trained 150 women to go out and use them.

We know now that radioactive material is very dangerous. But a hundred years ago, Marie worked almost around the clock in her shed without any protection at all. She even carried test tubes of radioactive isotopes in her pocket and kept them in her desk, liking the pretty blue-green light they gave off in the dark.

Marie Curie was the first woman to win the Nobel Prize and the only one to have won two. Her dedication and hard work meant that doctors have been able to help many thousands of ill and hurt people. But her research couldn't save her. She ended up dying of leukaemia – probably caused by radiation from the precious materials she worked with every day.

80

It's time you listened to me!

Finding your way around in the early days of sailing was all a bit hit and miss. Sailors needed a clock that was accurate enough to work out longitude at sea. But clocks in those days had pendulums, and the waves threw out the swing – and the time. With sailors getting lost all over the oceans, the English Parliament offered £20,000 as a reward for anyone who could find a solution.

Self-taught clockmaker John Harrison spent years of his life trying to make the perfect sea-going timekeeper. But to win the prize he had to get his ideas past the Board of Longitude – a group of very difficult scientists, some of them out to scoop the prize themselves . . .

The clock struck one Harrison's first clock didn't win the prize, but he thought he'd have another go.

The clock struck two With time ticking away, he started on his second clock – H2. But after discovering a design fault, he decided not to let it be tested at sea.

The clock struck three Harrison worked on his third timekeeper from 1740 to 1759. After nineteen years of labour, it didn't reach the accuracy required by the Board of Longitude.

The clock struck four Harrison's fourth timepiece – H4 – took six years to make and was better and smaller than anything else in the world. Harrison was

  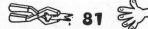

sixty-eight years old by then and had lost his sea legs, so in 1761 he sent his precious invention on its transatlantic trial in the care of his son William. When the ship reached Jamaica the watch was only five seconds out. A massive achievement!

When the ship returned, Harrison waited for the £20,000 prize – but the Board believed the results were just luck and demanded another trial. And another. And then some prototypes. Oh, and the designs and watches had to be handed over to the government. And so on ... It was only after the King became involved that Harrison got his money – nearly twelve years after H4 should have won the prize, and only a few years before he died!

A grand finale

It must be lovely being onstage with everyone cheering your wonderful performance again and again. But when you just fancy putting your feet up with a cup of tea, it could get a bit tiresome. So imagine taking 101 curtain calls, eighty (yes, really) minutes of clapping and one encore after another! That is exactly what the world famous tenor Placido Domingo had to put up with after singing in *Otello* in 1991. And how tough were the hands on that audience?

Weird!

Check your own endurance levels with our tough test

What's your idea of a fun place to stay on holiday?

a. A luxury hotel with a heated swimming pool and lots of fluffy towels

b. A caravan (as long as it's got its own indoor toilet and shower)

c. A tent with a campfire in a field full of cows

d. An activity camp with press-ups at dawn and a washing-up rota before bed at eight

What's the longest you've ever gone without chocolate?

a. Half an hour

b. One day

c. Two weeks, when Mum stopped my pocket money

d. I've never had chocolate, it's bad for you

You get a puncture when you are out cycling. Do you . . . ?

a. Get out your mobile and call your parent's five-star roadside-recovery service

b. Go to a phone box and call your dad to come and fix it for you

  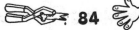

c. Get out your puncture kit, open it . . . and then call your dad

d. Get out your puncture kit and mend the hole in a few minutes – you like a challenge

What do you say when someone suggests a nice long walk on a rainy day?

a. I can't walk far; my legs feel like jelly

b. I'll catch up with you when my DVD finishes

c. All right, then – can I have something to eat on the way?

d. Nothing. You are too busy putting on your wet-weather gear

What do you do if you see an enormous spider in your bedroom?

a. Scream, run out and refuse to go back in until 'that thing' has been dealt with

b. Vacuum it up and leave Mum to do whatever she does with the bag

c. Get out your special spider catcher and gently put 'Leggy' outside into the garden

d. Pick it up barehanded and put it in the tank with your pet tarantula to see how they get on

How did you score?

Mostly a
Hopeless. Make sure you never get in any dangerous situations – ever.

Mostly b
Not bad. And with a bit of work you could build up to being pretty good.

Mostly c
Pretty good. You have real endurance potential.

Mostly d
Stop fibbing. In an endurance situation it's always better to stick with reality.

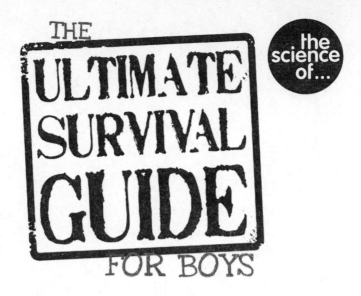

THE ULTIMATE SURVIVAL GUIDE FOR BOYS

the science of...

Mike Flynn

This book will teach you everything you need to know
to survive in the wilderness (or your back garden!)

Learn how to navigate by the stars, read a map, use
a compass, build a shelter, signal for help, find water,
leave tracking signs for others to follow and put
together the essential survival kit.

Take inspiration from the experts – find out how the
SAS approaches survival, how the Bedouin get by with
barely any water and how the Vikings used to navigate.

Read this book and you'll be prepared for
any eventuality!